CAREER AS A

COMPUTER SYSTEMS ANALYST

ONE OF THE HOTTEST CAREERS TODAY – and one with highly favorable job prospects for the foreseeable future – is computer systems analyst. Analysts are in high demand by organizations that use computers (and what company operates without a computer?). That means opportunities exist in virtually every business and government agency, in every industry around the world. Systems analysts earn good salaries and enjoy outstanding prospects for long-term advancement. They may work in safe, modern offices, travel around the country, or do their jobs from the comfort of their own homes. They play an important role in providing organizations with customized technical solutions to the most challenging issues.

Do you like working with computers? Do you enjoy solving mysteries and puzzles? Do you gain satisfaction from helping others? Are you a good communicator, both through the written word and while speaking with people? Do you like to learn new skills? Are you organized and responsible, and can you work well with others? Would you enjoy leading a team of colleagues towards successfully accomplishing an important goal? Then you may be ideally suited for a career as a systems analyst.

Computer systems analysts apply technology to solve problems for businesses and organizations of all sizes. Analysts may be involved in selecting new software and hardware for organizations, or they may work to make existing systems function more efficiently. They may modify current systems or plan new ones. Some analysts are experts in certain types of businesses, while others focus on the technical details of computer programs or physical equipment. All analysts stay busy determining how they can best apply technology to help their organizations resolve problems and take advantage of new opportunities.

The role of analysts is critical to helping their employers move forward with projects involving computer systems. They spend their time investigating issues by talking with everyone from high-ranking executives to data entry clerks. Computer analysts document their findings and propose solutions to address those issues. They remain heavily involved, while programmers, consultants and other information technology (IT) professionals implement the proposed solutions.

Many analysts focus on computer science while they are in college, particularly those who plan to work in highly technical fields. Such training is generally required for programmer-analysts, who perform the role of an analyst as well as programming computer languages. However, experience and training in technology are not mandatory to become a computer systems analyst. Many analysts are specialists in a certain industry (chemical manufacturing or banking, for example). These business-oriented analysts are more knowledgeable about the industry in which they work than with the technical details of the systems they work with. Still, analysts of all types must stay up to date on the latest technologies to ensure they can recommend the most practical and efficient solutions to the challenges their clients face.

If you have good analytical, technical and people skills, you can build a financially rewarding career as a computer systems analyst. With the right training and hard work, you can achieve the personal and professional satisfaction that comes with making organizations and individuals more productive and profitable.

WHAT YOU CAN DO NOW

EVEN WHILE YOU ARE STILL IN SCHOOL, there are several steps you can take to start preparing for a career as a computer systems analyst. Any courses directly related to technology and computers can help you gain in-depth familiarity with how systems work. Even though you will probably not be programming software, taking a class on computer programs will help you understand how data processing systems work. Math and business courses are useful, as you will need to understand basic business functions such as accounting and billing in order to analyze system changes. You will be using word processing, spreadsheets and other software as an analyst, so a basic keyboarding class is essential. If you are unable to find the right classes at your school, look at courses offered by a local college in such areas as computer design and systems architecture. Even certain non-credit courses can support your preparations.

Begin following practices used by professionals who are already employed in the field. Read industry periodicals, visit professional association websites and scan the business sections of newspapers to stay up to date with the computer industry. Attend local chapter meetings of professional groups and inquire about whether they have student memberships. Many such groups also offer scholarships, so getting involved in a professional association can help you improve your chances for those funding sources. Meeting professionals in the industry also helps you learn about internships and other opportunities to advance your career plans. If you already know what industry you want to work in – banking or telecommunications, for example – check into their associations and publications as well.

HISTORY OF THE CAREER

PRACTICAL, GENERAL USE COMPUTERS and the information technology profession have only existed since the middle part of the 20th century – although the field can trace its roots to the development of mathematics thousands of years ago. The first calculating machine was invented in 1623. Many other devices evolved throughout the Industrial Revolution.

Most of today's major IT companies began within the last 100 years. IBM was created as the Computing Tabulating Recording Company in 1911 through the merger of four other companies. IBM introduced the first electric typewriter in the 1930s and eventually dominated the computer world throughout the second half of the 20th century. Bell Labs, which was formed by AT&T in the 1920s, pioneered a number of innovations that drove the early days of the telecommunications industry. Hewlett-Packard (now HP) was founded in 1939 in a garage in Palo Alto, California, while Digital Equipment (DEC) began in 1958. Microsoft, launched in 1975, created early operating systems for the personal computer that helped it grow into a global industry leader.

The first general purpose computer, ENIAC, was developed in 1946 for the US Army. ENIAC covered more than 1,800 square feet of floor space and weighed 30 tons. While it was 1,000 times faster than earlier machines, ENIAC was programmed by manually wiring various switches. The computer's size and cost were also major shortcomings, with most of the early applications limited to government undertakings like the US space program.

UNIVAC, the first commercial computer, came in 1951 and cost some $1 million to construct. IBM introduced the first successful business computer in 1953 and launched the corporation nicknamed "Big Blue" towards becoming the largest computer company on the planet. These early computing platforms were large, complex, and expensive, requiring highly skilled engineers to keep them operating properly.

As the fledgling computer industry took root, the 1960s and 1970s saw a number of technological advances that reduced the size and cost of those early mainframe computers. Vacuum tubes and transistors were followed by integrated solid-state circuits and computer chips, so the size and cost of computers began to shrink. These innovative trends continued with the widespread adoption of personal computers in the 1980s, the World Wide Web in the 1990s, local computer networks, and a vast array of mobile computing devices such as "smart phones" earlier in this century. Those innovations made computers present in virtually all areas of our lives, from the cars we drive to classrooms to coffeemakers. The industry continues to seek smaller, faster and easier-to-use computing devices that bring convenience to consumers and businesses alike. Integrating those new computing platforms to interact efficiently and securely with the technical environments of businesses and governments continues to present challenges for computer systems analysts and other IT professionals.

During the computer revolution, software languages were introduced, replacing hard-wired computer instructions with "soft" programs that are stored temporarily as bits and bytes in the computer's memory. Computers during the early 1950s were programmed using machine languages, which are similar to the instructions a computer uses internally to control its functions. These early languages were extremely technical in nature and required highly-trained engineers to write the programs. By the early 1960s, a newer generation of languages such as COBOL and FORTRAN evolved. While these languages still required skilled programmers, the commands were closer to the English language, so they were easier for technicians to learn code and debug than their predecessors. Computer programming languages continue to evolve today, allowing non-technical users to more easily understand and control what instructions are being given to a system. Since analysts may be called upon to review computer code, the evolution of more English-like languages makes it easier for analysts to understand how a particular system works.

Innovations in how computers present information to users have also made systems easier to use. Systems from the 1950s through the early 1970s were controlled by punched cards – 80-column pieces of stiff paper that contained coded instructions in a hexadecimal format. The output from a computer system was typically only available through paper printouts. Punched cards were soon followed by video display terminals (VDTs), which allowed programmers and non-technical staff to input data through a keyboard and receive results on their screens. By the late 1980s, VDTs generally gave way to "smart terminals" – personal computers, notebooks and tablets attached to a network that do more of their own processing and provide data on colorful, multi-media user-friendly platforms.

As computers have evolved over the last century, the industry has moved away from its heavy reliance on strictly technical personnel. This presents more opportunities for the computer systems analyst – someone who generally focuses more on the business and practical applications of technology, rather than the technical details of making the computer run. Analysts may have a strong technical background, or they may be more oriented towards how a business runs. Either way, their primary role is to provide their clients and employers with the best use of computer technology.

WHERE YOU WILL WORK

COMPUTERS ARE USED TODAY throughout all industries, across the country and around the world, in organizations large and small, and in the business, government, military and nonprofit sectors. Every organization has computers, and most of those organizations need systems analysts. Even a small business that uses only networked personal computers for e-commerce or word processing will occasionally need the services of a systems analyst to review its operations and suggest improvements.

There is a large concentration of computer systems analyst jobs within the information technology industry itself. Companies that make hardware and software, or that provide consulting services to their clients, hire analysts who can maximize the effective use of their products. However, every sector of society relies on IT services, so retailers, manufacturers, universities, banks, oil companies, hospitals, airlines, architectural firms, scientific laboratories, entertainment companies, sports teams, and government agencies can all provide career paths for analysts.

The industries with the highest employment levels of computer systems analysts are:

Computer systems design and related services

Management of companies and enterprises

Insurance carriers

Data processing, hosting and related services

State government

Software publishers

Computer and peripheral equipment manufacturers

Regardless of what industry an analyst works in, the individual will usually work from an office building. Some analysts are located in computer labs and IT departments, while others may work in a specific business unit, such as accounting or marketing. At some companies, analysts and other staff work from home, using remote computer access, conference calls and videoconferencing to stay in touch with project team members. Those employed by an insurance company, on the other hand, will probably work from one main office at the firm's headquarters.

Analysts who work for organizations that provide software, hardware or consulting services may be required to travel extensively. Clients of these IT vendors are scattered across many geographic regions. Analysts must regularly meet with these clients. Usually those meetings are at the client's office, not at your company headquarters. Sometimes these visits require brief overnight trips. For other projects, consultants may spend months at the client's location and only return home on the weekends.

Some analysts enjoy being "road warriors" and traveling extensively, while others prefer staying close to home and only taking occasional excursions. Whatever your preference, there are sure to be opportunities as a computer systems analyst to find a work arrangement that fits your preferences and lifestyle.

THE WORK YOU WILL DO

THE BASIC ROLE OF A COMPUTER systems analyst is determining how to best use computers to solve an organization's problems or enhance its opportunities to grow. Analysts analyze issues and find ways to use computer technology to tackle challenges in business, scientific, nonprofit, military and government settings. They may recommend buying new hardware and software to address an organization's needs, or they may recommend ways to modify existing systems to address new requirements.

Computer systems analysts work in a wide variety of organizations, including large corporations, small businesses, government agencies, and academia. They are employed in great numbers by government agencies, insurance and financial services companies, computer hardware and software firms, and equipment manufacturers. However, since computers are used in all industries, systems analysts are found in virtually every sector of the economy.

Analysts may work under a variety of titles, which generally reflect the specific focus of their roles. Specific types of analysts include:

Business Systems Analyst

Also known as a business analyst or BA, user analyst, or simply analyst, this professional must have a mix of expertise in how a business operates and systems knowledge. In other words, the BA must know what the business wants to accomplish and how a computer system can best support those needs. The BA is often the go-between who conveys the organization's goals to the programming staff.   While other types of analysts are primarily IT specialists, the BA is more an expert on how the business works from a non-technical standpoint.

Documentation Analyst

Also called technical writer or technical author, this analyst creates various documents that explain how an organization's systems operate and how they should function in the new or modified environment that a proposed project will put in place.

Operational Analyst or Production Analyst

They focus on the technical aspects of making computer hardware and software systems operate more efficiently.

Programmer-Analyst

This is a group of systems developers who have the roles of computer programmer as well as analyst. Typically a programmer-analyst is primarily a person who is familiar with computer programs, but also does some analysis as part of programming duties.

Software Quality Assurance Analyst (QA) or Test Analyst

These analysts test new software or changes being made to existing systems. They develop plans for testing system modifications, make sure the system operates as designed, and work with programmers and other IT professionals to make corrections. Like a BA, a QA needs considerable business knowledge to make sure the system changes meet the organization's needs.

System Architect, System Designer, and Information Systems Analysts

They all specialize in selecting and structuring the right systems for a specific organization's needs. In some organizations, the title systems analyst is also used for employees who focus exclusively on the computer system itself.

While these specific types of analysts may specialize in a specific part of the business or technical environment, many tasks are the same for all computer systems analysts. The analyst is usually called upon when a company, government office or other organization is considering either modifying the current system or installing a new system. There can be many reasons for these changes, including new government regulations, the introduction of new products, making an old system easier to use, or simply upgrading to a newer, more efficient system.

Software development life cycle

The process of translating business requirements into computer processing results is called the software development life cycle. The analyst is typically the starting point for a process that involves a team of programmers, testers, business experts and other knowledgeable staff from throughout the company. Each new project typically has a temporary team of employees (and, in some cases, outside consultants) who come together for the duration of a specific undertaking. The analyst may lead the project team. However, even when there is a professional project manager assigned to head the team, the analyst often plays the lead role in moving tasks forward.

The first step in the process is for the analyst to research how the system currently operates and how the new (or modified) system should operate in the future. Analysts begin by reviewing and documenting their existing knowledge about how the present system works. They may supplement that knowledge by reading previous system documentation, talking to programmers, and testing the system in a controlled environment.

More time is generally spent determining how the business units want the new system to work. Analysts interview business managers about what their goals are for the proposed changes. They hold meetings with clerks, supervisors and others who work with the system on a daily basis. If the change is being driven by new government regulations, they may talk with the company's lawyers to make sure the business complies with the new rules.

Joint application development sessions

Often the analyst will bring all these parties together to discuss the system changes. This ensures that all divisions within the business and all levels of company personnel agree on the goals of the system change. These meetings, called joint application development (JAD) sessions, are a major source of information for analysts. During the JAD sessions, the analyst simply listens to the points presented, probes to fully understand the issues, and identifies areas that will need to be clarified. The analyst generally makes no recommendations at this time. The immediate goal is simply understanding the needs and expectations of the company's various departments.

Recommendations

After gathering as much information as possible, the next step is to organize and analyze this data to determine the optimal solution to the challenges the project will address. The analyst will also document the findings of the JAD sessions and other investigations through notes, charts and similar media. The documentation is distributed to the attendees for review, modification and final approval.

Analysts must also review alternatives and make recommendations for system changes. They must consider the costs of various options, such as enhancing an existing system versus buying new software from a vendor, or having the company's IT staff build a system from scratch. An analyst must also consider whether a proposed solution is technically feasible in the current environment, or whether new hardware might be required.

Once the business requirements are completed, the next step is translating those needs into computer system requirements. The analyst works directly with the programming staff to determine whether the current system can be modified. If not, new software and/or hardware will be required to make the project successful. Other considerations include:

Documenting feasible alternatives

There are often multiple approaches to address a given situation. The analyst must sort through these options, identify the pros and cons to each method, and make recommendations to upper management on the optimal solution to a given situation.

Identifying the expected costs and anticipated benefits of various options

The least expensive alternative may not be the best solution. Analysts must prepare a cost/benefit analysis that shows the benefits and expenses that would accrue from the proposed solutions. They may also document the expected return on investment for the system changes under consideration.

Ensuring that the new or modified system will be as easy to learn and use as possible

System changes that make any employee's daily job more difficult, cause errors or require longer to accomplish tasks, will not be viewed as successes.

Making sure the changes follow company policies and procedures

The analyst will present proposed system changes. The proposal is then reviewed, amended and eventually approved by the departments represented at the JAD session, as well as the IT staff.

Programming and Testing

At this point, the programmers – either internal company staff or IT professionals from an outside vendor – will turn the plans developed by the analyst into specifications for creating computer code. Once the programming specs are completed, the group charged with testing the system changes will draw on documents from the analyst and the programmers to develop a plan for testing the new system. The analyst is often called upon to answer questions, modify proposed solutions and resolve conflicts that arise during the programming and testing phases of the project.

Once testing is completed and the IT staff is ready to implement the system changes, the analyst may also be involved in helping educate the business units on how the new system will work. If the company has a training department, the analyst will work with the professional educational staff to develop classes and how-to documentation for the businesspeople who will use the new system. If there is no training unit, the analyst may prepare and present the training classes. Once the system "goes live," the analyst answers questions and resolves any issues that are found.

Analysts also have duties beyond a specific project (or projects, as most analysts will work on multiple projects at the same time). They may be called upon to use their business expertise to help resolve daily issues or train new personnel. They may also field questions from programmers who need to better understand how the business works. They may also be involved in planning and budgeting meetings with executives as they consider future projects.

Systems analysts must also find time to stay on top of the newest technological advances that could benefit their business units. They also need to stay up to date on the latest trends for their industry and on government regulations that may affect their company's operations.

While the analyst is responsible for performing or leading a variety of tasks, the ultimate goal remains the same: using computer systems to solve problems in the most efficient manner possible to support an organization's goals.

COMPUTER SYSTEMS ANALYSTS TELL THEIR OWN STORIES

I Am a Business Systems Analyst

"I began my professional career in the 1970s, when computers were just gaining wide acceptance in the business world. My uncle had graduated from college with a degree in agriculture, but decided to get into the computer industry in the 1960s. After working his way up the ladder as a programmer/analyst, he eventually became president of a company that provided IT services to electrical cooperatives throughout the southeastern United States. As there was little advice available for the industry at this early stage, he gave me plenty of pointers on what courses to take and how to build an IT career.

In 1974, I obtained a two-year Associate of Science degree from the community college in my hometown, a city of about 50,000 people in Tennessee. There were only three industries in that town with computer jobs: the college, three banks and an insurance company. I applied at the insurance company, as my father had been an insurance salesman for many years and I had some business knowledge that helped me get my foot in the door. I worked at that company for two years as a computer programmer and analyst.

However, as there were limited career opportunities in my hometown, I decided to move to Atlanta, Georgia, where there were numerous insurance companies and not enough experienced technical staff. I worked for several financial companies, gradually working my way up to positions of increasing responsibility. Over time, I was drawn away from the programming positions into roles that called for strictly analytical skills. Computer programming languages and systems change rapidly, so it was challenging staying current with the latest technology. Analysts must also constantly refresh their skills, but they do not need as much in-depth technical knowledge of computer languages as programmers do.

By the 1990s, I found that my lack of a four-year degree made it more difficult to change jobs or gain promotions from existing employers. So I went back to school at night, completing my bachelor's degree through a university extension program. The four-year degree in applied sciences, with a concentration in computer science and financial services, made me more marketable to employers. I also obtained several insurance industry designations which enhanced my employment prospects and the ability to do my job once I was hired. Part of my success can be attributed to being a "life learner" – continuing to learn about my industry and about new technology to support my career well beyond college.

My career as a business systems analyst in the insurance industry has spanned 30 years now. I began working with punch card systems, progressing through VDTs to workstations, laptops and the Internet. Staying current with ever-changing technology remains a constant challenge throughout my career. The payoff for me comes from using technology to help solve problems and to make life easier for my colleagues in the insurance industry. I gain a great satisfaction from helping others."

I Manage a Team of Computer Analysts

"I began my career as a computer programmer/analyst after receiving a Bachelor of Science degree in computer science. Early on, I was drawn more to the analytical side of the industry: working with non-technical staff to understand their challenges, suggesting ways technology could help solve their problems, and seeing those proposals move from idea to reality. My career soon focused more on analysis and less on programming, so I took a position as a computer systems analyst with a software company. Soon I decided to focus exclusively on computer analyst opportunities in the software field.

After several years as an analyst, I felt I was ready to take on more responsibility. I volunteered for semi-management positions, such as lead analyst working alongside a team of several other staff. As I was given more management responsibilities, I realized I needed formal management training so I could move into supervisory roles with more responsibility. I enrolled in a part-time degree program and obtained a master's degree in management. Soon afterwards, a management position came open at the software company where I worked, and I was promoted to that job. I now manage a team of 12 other analysts. We provide support both for internal projects (such as an upgrade to an existing software package) and for external clients who hire us to analyze their business needs and suggest computer-based solutions.

While I no longer do the analysis myself, my years as an analyst allow me to more effectively coach and manage my staff. Most of my time is spent on helping my team of analysts work more effectively and efficiently. My experience as an analyst helps me lead them through difficult situations with clients. I enjoy hiring new employees and training them to become better analysts.

Like many IT professionals, I have changed jobs and companies several times over my career. While I am happy today at my current position, I am always open to new opportunities that may be on the horizon. I know my solid background as an analyst and my management skills will keep me marketable to potential employers. I am always looking for new challenges and opportunities to grow."

I Am a Systems Analyst Working as an Independent IT Consultant

"When I began my career in information technology, I did not imagine that I would eventually own my own consulting business. I majored in computer science in college with a focus on systems analysis. After graduation I landed a job as a systems analyst with the IT department at a bank. I stayed there for two years before moving on to another bank. Like many IT professionals, I typically stayed with an employer for two to three years before moving on to new challenges with a different company. The IT career path often sees analysts, programmers and other technical workers changing jobs every few years to gain broader experience, learn new technologies, and increase their salaries.

During those years of climbing the career ladder, I have met many contract IT professionals who either work for large consulting companies or on their own. They may   work for a company under a six-month contract, or their engagements could extend for many years. Some consultants work in their home towns, while others travel across the country – or around the world – on assignment. The contrast flow of new challenges and new opportunities working with a variety of clients appeals to me.

My first step into consulting was to work for an IT professional services company. These companies specialize in matching skilled IT workers with the needs of their clients for short- and medium-term engagements. Contracts lasting six to 12 months are the norm for the industry, with these temporary workers moving on to new clients when their projects are completed. I worked for a contract labor service for three years while I learned the ropes of the business. I eventually decided that a life of constant change best suits my personality and lifestyle.

Since that time, I have gone into business for myself. I use my previous experience and contacts to find additional work in the financial services sector. While I do enjoy the constant flow of new opportunities and the occasional travel, running my own company does present a number of challenges. There are a number of activities that require your time beyond your daily work as an analyst. You also have to:

Find prospective new clients and market your services to them. Charge your clients competitive fees that provide a salary for yourself, cover expenses that employers typically take care of (like health insurance), and pay for the administrative costs than any business incurs.

Negotiate contract terms with prospective clients, and have those contracts drafted or reviewed by your attorney.

Keep financial records for the business. You will be responsible for filing your own taxes, or for hiring an accountant to handle those details.

Later, if your business grows large enough for you to add additional contract staff, your business life gets more complex. You will have to keep up with their contracts, cover an employer's portion of their taxes, possibly provide insurance and other benefits, and ensure that you comply with local and federal labor laws. You   may need to obtain office space for your enterprise, and you may end up spending more time managing your staff and your business than doing what you really like – being a computer systems analyst.

For reasons such as these, I have decided to remain a one person operation. I spend most of my time working as a systems analyst for various clients, which keeps the amount of extra administrative work to a minimum. By only having to keep myself busy with paying contracts, I can focus on finding the most challenging and rewarding assignments that keep me interested."

PERSONAL QUALIFICATIONS

BECOMING A SUCCESSFUL COMPUTER systems analyst requires a combination of technical knowledge (also called "hard skills) and personal attributes ("soft skills"). While basic technical skills can be learned in school, other personal traits come into play that can mean the difference between a rewarding career and a work life filled with frustration.

The title "analyst" emphasizes the importance of analytical skills in this career. In order to analyze a situation and propose the best solution, an analyst needs to be a problem solver. If you like figuring out puzzles or finding the most efficient ways to get things done, this could be the job for you.

Analysts also must be comfortable digging into the details of a challenge, keeping track of large amounts of data, and recording their findings and recommendations. Much of an analyst's job involves creating documentation – how the system works today, how it needs to work tomorrow, and the best way to move from the current situation to an optimal environment in the future. An analyst's work provides the basis for programmers and other technical staff to evaluate their options and make changes to the system to support the business case for a given project. If you leave out important details – such as the need for the company's new billing system to process credit cards – it can cost the company thousands of dollars correcting the oversight.

Aside from these "hard skills," an analyst needs to be proficient at working with and communicating with people. While the field may appear to be a mostly technical one, people skills are essential for success. In this career, you will be interviewing subject matter experts from all areas of the company – anyone from a call center clerk to a vice president – about proposed systems changes. You will lead meetings attended by business and technical staff to discuss the details of a project. You will document your findings and recommendations, distribute that to all interested parties, and make corrections and changes based on the feedback you receive. This requires the analyst to be a good listener, a good communicator and a group discussion leader. While you may not aspire to become a manager, you will still need to be a good manager of time, resources and sometimes other people – even those from other departments who you do not formally supervise.

In addition, you will need to enjoy learning. Life means constant change, and a life in technology requires ongoing education. You will certainly need to keep pace with new technical advances. However, you will also be challenged to learn new software to do your job, new practices and procedures in the IT development process, new regulations that govern your industry, new products and services that your company introduces, and other aspects of a company's environment that change constantly. Being an analyst requires staying up to date with all the factors that affect your job responsibilities.

ATTRACTIVE FEATURES

COMPUTER SYSTEMS ANALYST CONSISTENTLY ranks among the top five "hot" careers for the next decade – as high as second in some surveys. The growth, earnings, creative and personal potential in this career seem unlimited as the computer revolution shows no signs of slowing down. Opportunities are wide open to work in a broad range of industries for large public corporations, private employers, government agencies and nonprofit institutions.

If you like learning new skills and challenging yourself to solve problems, you will never be bored as a systems analyst. You will work on a variety of unique projects. The pace of the work is different from one job to the next. The IT field continues to evolve with innovative software and cutting-edge hardware breakthroughs, so computer analysts are always busy staying up to date with the newest developments.

You will work with intelligent experts in a number of technical and general fields as you help guide important projects from concept to reality. The work you do will have a positive impact on your organization, your community and the people who live there. Your success can bring financial rewards, personal fulfillment and satisfaction from a job well done.

The working conditions for computer systems analysts are among the best in the white-collar world. Major companies provide competitive salaries, attractive benefits, state-of-the-art equipment, in-house training, and other perks to lure the top candidates to their IT shops. Most offer a career path towards advancement, with greater responsibilities and rewards whether you remain an analyst or possibly move into management. Extra amenities like gymnasiums, game rooms, company picnics and retreats, holiday parties, and comfortable, clean offices help boost morale and productivity.

Computer systems analysts are also highly respected by their peers and clients. Analysts work closely with employees in other departments at all levels of the organization, to implement a new computer system or improve an existing one. Those employees – from hourly clerks to the executive suite – appreciate professionals who make their lives easier when a successful project delivers quality results that help them meet their company goals.

If you have an entrepreneurial personality, a career as an analyst can also pave the way for you to open your own business. Many analysts and other IT professionals begin their working lives as employees of other companies before striking out on their own. After they build up a body of knowledge, experience, and contacts, they become independent contractors – either working for themselves or through one of the many IT job placement services that connect analysts with employers who need qualified professionals. Contractors enjoy the challenges that come with keeping pace with new technology. Best of all, they prefer being in charge of their own careers.

Whether you decide to climb the corporate ladder or follow an independent path, a career as a computer systems analyst can be both financially and personally rewarding throughout your lifetime.

UNATTRACTIVE FEATURES

WHILE A CAREER AS A SYSTEMS ANALYST can bring great rewards, it can also be stressful. Your clients may be internal (fellow employees of your company) or external (such as the users of software packages your company sells). Those clients have high expectations that you can solve their problems quickly, efficiently – and at little or no cost to them. However, a complex issue can take a great deal of time to solve. The solution may cost more to implement or take longer to resolve than clients want. Sometimes, there are problems that cannot be solved because of technical or procedural constraints. In those cases, the relationship between the IT staff and their clients can become strained.

At various times during the project life cycle, analysts and other IT professionals may work more than 40 hours a week – particularly when deadlines approach or the project is not going smoothly. Most analysts are paid a set annual salary rather than by the hour, so there is no overtime pay when analysts work beyond the traditional workweek. In addition, analysts may be "on call" at night or over the weekend in case there are problems with system modifications.

For some analysts, the constant demands for continuing education can be daunting. Hardware, software and the methods for running projects are constantly changing, which requires ongoing training to keep pace with the latest breakthroughs. Many employers do offer training courses to help you keep pace. However, even when the classes are given during working hours, your job responsibilities continue, so you may end up working outside normal business hours to keep your work moving forward on schedule. Training and research may happen on your own time rather than during company hours.

A computer systems analyst's work is complex and can become exhausting. Project life cycles can last many months or even years. Lengthy projects can bring personal stress, conflicts with co-workers and even burnout. Explaining complex ideas and solutions can be frustrating when other team members have trouble understanding your proposals. It can also be disappointing when your suggestions are not accepted by your peers or clients. Sometimes a new project begins before a previous project ends, so you may be juggling multiple tasks at the same time. Every project includes numerous meetings, so your schedule is always full – and always subject to change when a crisis requires immediate attention. There can be pressure from demanding managers, colleagues who are not team players, and clients who constantly criticize.

Becoming a successful systems analyst requires patience, creativity, self-discipline, being able to see things from another's point of view – and a thick skin.

EDUCATION AND TRAINING

AS RECENTLY AS THE 1980S, COMPUTER systems analysts and other IT professionals could start their careers with little or no formal training. Many of today's successful analysts began with only an associate degree from a community college, a computer-related certification from a vocational school – or little more than a good head for numbers and a willingness to learn. Others had degrees in mathematics, engineering or the physical sciences.

Vocational and technical schools, community colleges and technical training institutions still offer programs lasting one to two years that provide a basic education in computer science. However, over the last 30 years, educational institutions have built extensive degree programs around the IT discipline. Today most employers expect analysts to complete four years of college and earn a bachelor's degree to obtain an entry-level position. Experience in the industry is required to move up to more senior positions. A master's degree is required for positions of responsibility at the executive level. A master's may also be needed in certain highly specialized industries (such as scientific research) or in positions of a highly complex technical nature.

Most analysts have degrees in one of the many computer science disciplines. However, those who choose to focus on a certain industry may have degrees related to that business. Most degree programs today include a sizeable number of computer-related courses as part of their normal curriculum. For example, a person earning a degree in finance will also take classes which present technology from a business standpoint. If you have a finance degree and an aptitude for technology, you can become a systems analyst for an insurance company, for you will possess insights into both the IT and the business aspects.

Universities offer information technology degrees under a number of schools. The programs may be in the departments of computer science, management information systems, business information systems or software engineering. Courses can include specific programming languages, systems design, software development, Internet-specific applications, databases and IT management.

The majority of accredited colleges and universities offer degrees in computer science. According to a recent survey, these are the top schools for computer science degrees:

Carnegie Mellon University

Massachusetts Institute of Technology

Stanford University

Cornell University

University of Illinois – Urbana-Champaign

University of Washington

Princeton University

University of Texas – Austin

Georgia Institute of Technology

Students planning a career as a computer systems analyst can expect to take a mixture of technical and general courses. While they may not be required to learn a programming language, such a class can help the potential analyst better understand computer systems and the challenges programmers face implementing the analyst's ideas. Classes include systems analysis and design, concepts of information systems, business systems, database fundamentals, computer networking, working with Internet applications, and the basics of operating systems.

Students can also expect general courses in business principals, mathematics, and the humanities.

Beyond a college degree, certification programs are common within the IT industry as a way to illustrate knowledge and keep skills current. Certification is not typically required for business analysts, although it may be expected in certain industries. For example, someone who works with stocks and bonds may be required to obtain certain licenses from the Securities and Exchange Commission. Certification is more commonly expected for those who work in highly technical jobs, such as programmer/analysts. For example, certification in Microsoft, Linux or UNIX operating systems may be required of those who work closely with those technologies. Certifications can be obtained from private training centers and often through public colleges.

Studying for certifications also provides a way for analysts and other IT professionals to keep current on the latest advances in technology, analytical practices and business developments. While a certificate may not be required to obtain an entry-level job, it could be a prerequisite for advancing within a company or moving to a new position after you gain experience. Continuing education through seminars, online courses and self-paced study is provided by employers; by public colleges and private training companies; professional societies like the Institute of Electronic and Electrical Engineers (IEEE) Computer Society, and vendors of software and hardware products. Most companies will provide internal training or reimburse employees for approved external training programs that directly relate to the employee's current job or career path.

EARNINGS

THE CURRENT AVERAGE ANNUAL salary of a computer systems analyst is about $85,000. That average represents a slight increase over $80,000 two years ago, and a significant jump from $75,000 four years ago. More recent surveys by various private recruiting services show similar trends that indicate average salaries continue to rise – even during the recent economic downturn.

Starting salaries for entry level computer systems analysts naturally will be lower than the industry average. However, even the lowest 10 percent of analysts earn about $50,000, while those in the bottom 25 percent are   paid $65,000. At the other end of the spectrum, experienced analysts in the 90 percentile earn $125,000 or more, according to government statistics.

Earnings for systems analysts vary by geographic region, industry and local economic factors. The industries with the top-paying analyst salaries are in the energy sector, specifically mining support activities, and oil and gas extraction. Other high earnings industries are satellite telecommunications; manufacturing magnetic and optical media; and healthcare and pharmaceuticals.

Candidates considering job opportunities should also look at other factors in addition to salary when evaluating competing offers of employment. Benefits can vary widely from company to company. In a large corporation, the value of benefits can total 30 percent of the base salary. Company benefits package may include medical, life and other insurance coverage; paid time off for vacation, holidays or sick leave; pensions and other retirement-oriented features; and opportunities to buy company stock.

OPPORTUNITIES

THE CAREER OUTLOOK FOR THE computer systems analyst field continues to be strong for the foreseeable future. Job prospects should be generally excellent. Because these professionals are usually required to be accessible to their employer's or client's place of business, it is less likely that systems analysts will be off-shored than other IT occupations which can be performed completely via computer and the Internet.

There are approximately 500,000 persons employed as computer systems analysts. That total is more than one percent higher than the work force total just a year ago, indicating that the need for analysts continues to grow – even during tough economic times that have reduced employment in many fields. The National Employment Matrix forecasts a 20 percent growth in the field, with employment projected to reach 600,000 by 2018.

With the usage of computers expanding every day, there are opportunities for systems analysts across the country. Many opportunities are with major corporations, which tend to locate their headquarters in larger states and cities. The five states with the highest employment levels for computer systems analysts are California, Texas, Virginia, New York and New Jersey. The metropolitan areas with the largest concentrations of analysts are Washington DC, New York/New Jersey, Atlanta, Dallas, Chicago, Houston and Los Angeles.

Working for a corporation does not necessarily mean moving to a large city. Some companies embrace telecommuting – working from one's home or another remote location rather than being in the same office building with one's colleagues. Multinational corporations like IBM that have "gone virtual" find that employees are happier and more productive working from home instead of driving to an office each day. Companies also reduce costs by using telecommuting. There is almost always a need for some face-to-face meetings and on-site inspections.

As computers continue to penetrate more industries and smaller companies, there are opportunities for analysts to work with small and medium-sized companies in suburban settings, smaller towns and even rural areas. The Internet, social media and other technologies allow more companies of all sizes to move further away from concentrated urban areas without negatively impacting the goods and services they provide.

In a similar fashion, there will also be more opportunities for entrepreneurial systems analysts to go into business for themselves as consultants. Being able to work for yourself – to pick your clients, set your working hours, and travel as much or as little as you desire – enables many analysts to focus on the opportunities that provide them the right balance of financial reward and personal satisfaction.

GETTING STARTED

IF A CAREER AS A COMPUTER SYSTEMS analyst sounds attractive, there is no better time to start preparing than today. The more information you can gather as soon as possible, the better decision you can make on your future direction. This enables you to take the proper steps now to be ready for the future.

The best approach is the same methodology a computer systems professional uses to tackle a project: gather information, analyze your findings, and come to a decision.

Written information about computer careers is widely available. The libraries at your school and in your community have books, magazines and other resources with information about the profession. Even the business section of your newspaper contains articles on general economic trends, or what areas local companies are targeting for future growth. The Internet has a broad range of easily accessible information provided by professional associations, government agencies, industry recruiters, private companies, and universities. College catalogs and websites contain valuable data about courses and degrees, enabling you to select the right program to support your goals.

Talk to individuals in your chosen field. Professionals who are working as analysts or with them (such as managers or recruiters) can supply up-to-date information about the current state of the industry and informed predictions of its future development. You can find such individuals through local chapters of professional organizations, or by contacting companies in your area with large IT departments. Some professional groups have outreach programs that target interested students, while others allow you to attend their meetings at a discounted rate. Also, discuss your plans with your school counselor for insight into the current job market, potential internships, and educational opportunities in your area. Last but certainly not least, get input from family and friends on how well they believe this career fits your personality and your strengths.

After you gather and organize your information, give serious thought to whether a career as a systems analyst sounds right for you. Do you feel you could meet the educational requirements and develop the required technical skills? Do you like working with people to identify and solve their problems? How are your communication skills – written, verbal and one-on-one with others? But most importantly, can you see yourself happy and successful in a career as a computer systems analyst?

If you decide this is the right choice for you, start making preparations to choose the right college program to get you started on your way. The computer industry has been growing for decades and the outlook is even brighter today. Becoming a computer systems analyst can open the door to fulfilling opportunities and rewards that lie ahead.

ASSOCIATIONS

■ **American Society of Information Science**
www.asis.org

■ **Association for Computing Machinery**
www.acm.org

■ **Association of Information Technology Professionals**
www.aitp.org

■ **Independent Computer Consultant Association**
www.icca.org

■ **Institute for Certification of Computing Professionals**
www.iccp.org

■ **National Association of Computer Consultant Businesses**
www.naccb.org

■ **Society of Computer Professionals**
www.comprof.org

■ **Society for Information Management**
www.simnet.org

■ **The IEEE Society**
www.computer.org

PERIODICALS

■ **ComputerWorld**
www.computerworld.com

■ **Datamation**
www.datamation.com

■ **Doctor Dobb's Journal**
www.drdobbs.com

■ **IEEE Xplore**
www.ieeexplore.ieee.org

■ **Information Today**
www.infotoday.com

■ **Information Week**
www.informationweek.com

■ **InfoWorld**
www.infoworld.com

WEBSITES

■ **CareerBuilder**
www.careerbuilder.com

■ **Dice**
www.dice.com

■ **Modern Analyst**
www.modernanalyst.com

■ **Monster**
www.monster.com

www.ingramcontent.com/pod-product-compliance
Lightning Source LLC
LaVergne TN
LVHW052126070326
832902LV00038B/3968